Homecoming
A Journey to Light

a collection of poetry

Dr. Makeba Morgan Hill

ISBN: 9798218130350 (Paperback)

ISBN: 9798218130367 (Ebook)

Illustrator: Oeindrilla Mukherjee (@artsyticc)

Book Design by HMDpublishing

Dedication

Parents are our first teachers. Cherish them, flaws and all.

This book of poetry is dedicated to my parents: the late Carl W. Morgan, also known as, Abdul Hasib Matin (God rest his soul), and Beverly Morgan, my Earth angel.

Among other things, my father was a poet and a teacher. He encouraged me to write and I'm glad I listened. My mother was also a teacher, but above all, she was a nurturing provider. She is still a rock upon which I firmly stand. I am grateful for them.

I love you both to Infinity and the Great Beyond!

Contents

Epigraph

Love is not for the faint of heart;
it is for the strong and mighty.
The only way to light is love.
God is Love.

-Dr. Makeba Morgan Hill

Preface
Finding Makeba

My Journey

Days rolled by
Months elapsed
Years passed

I remember

Living day to day
Longing for more
Learning through it all

I prayed

A pilgrimage home
A spark of joy
A flicker of hope

Ignited

Living
Laughing
Loving

Blessed

May I choose the right path, Almighty God, turning from what I know you would not have me do in order to pursue what is fitting in your sight. Guide me through your undying love and your knowing words. Allow me to see, to hear, to feel, to know, and to trust, Father God. I ask this in your holy name.

Amen

PART 1.
Living

*This journey called life is not easy,
but that is part of the fun.*

01 | *Time*

Time concerns me in this journey called life.

Some time, no time, hard time, in time,
On time, timeless, timely,
Running out of time!
What does it mean?

Is time relative or is time real?
Can time really heal all things?
Could it be that it doesn't really mean a thing?

I guess time will tell...

02 | *Imagine*

Imagine realizing after all this time
that you were holding your breath.

That tightness in your chest.
That veil over your eyes.
That not quite fully happy feeling
What is that?

You were holding your breath. For years!
Did you even know?

You were comfortable
You were fine
Hell, you were living
But something was not quite right

Was it too much to ask
to feel how you felt
when you felt
how you felt before...?
Remember that song?

Imagine finally taking a breath.
A breath so deep it scares you.
Are you ok?

Those worrisome first breaths
Irregular...chest aching
Strange. Wait... Your heart beats!

Skin-tingling. Hair-raising. Spine-chilling.
The release. Uncharted. Exhilarating.

Breathe in. Breathe out

My God!

Never stop breathing again...

03 | *Pittsburgh, ATL*

I belong here
This is mine
We are family
All of the time

The common thread
The tie that binds
It's our community
And it's our time to shine

Overlooked
Misunderstood
Devalued
Abused

Strong and mighty
When united
We, the people
Will never be defeated

04 | *Taco Tuesday*

There's nothing quite like a dollop of guacamole
on a warm, crunchy taco
on a cold winter's night.

Fiesta music playing
to add a little flair,
Margaritas flowing and
the smell of lime lingers in the air

Taco Tuesday, you say?
I say tacos every day!
Arriba!

05 | *Abyss*

I look into his eyes,
searching...
He averts my gaze.

I place his hand under my dress
on the skin of my bare waist.
TV glaring, he's in a daze.
There's nothing.

Has time quieted the flame
or was there never one to claim?
I'm just amazed.

But now I know—
there's nothing.

Is there room to improve?
Am I to live the rest of my life
in search of my groove?

I'm pissed—
there's nothing.

Time wasted, but why?
Still searching;
I try.
All these years,
was it worth it?
I simply don't know.

But what I do know
What I know for sure...
there's nothing.

Absolutely nothing.

06 | *Tears*

Tears well in my eyes
as I ponder the missteps of our past,
as I worry about the decisions of today,
as I revel in knowing what is right,
while rushing to protect my fragile heart

Tears flow down my face
as I mourn what once was,
as I celebrate the good times,
as I thank you for all that you've given me,
while I struggle to suture this fresh wound

My tears fall to the earth,
but as they do,
I recognize the gift...

We are alive
We are free
I am you
You are me
Always

07 | Spring

Birds are chirping
The sky is bluer
My nose is itching
Spring flowers in bloom

Eminent warm weather
Outdoor dining
Friends and fellowship
Bring glad tidings

A season of new life
A rebirth of sorts
Springtime is on its way
Enjoy it, folks!

08 | *Natural High*

Clear sky
Brisk air
Your face

Afrobeats
Sweet treats
Christmas trees

Good books
Cat naps
Sunshine

Private jokes
Belly laughs
Slow dance

Long walks
Barbecue
Me with you

09 | Fantasy vs. Reality

Tell me your fantasies and
I'll tell you mine, in time.
Once we establish your intentions,
I may be inclined to more freely define
Just what it is that is on my mind.

Can I trust you with my deepest thoughts and dreams,
my wishes, and my fantasies?
You say my wish is your command.
Is that true or will we just continue to do what we do?

The thought of you takes me back to
my childhood fantasies.
My happily ever after.
How sad...
This state of affairs we're in.

10 | *War*

This fighting must stop.
The division must end.
What has come of this world we are in?
What happened to us?
Where is the love?
Grab your kids and give them a hug.
This is not how it's supposed to be.
We will soon see.
Very soon we will all be free.

11 | Together

I see the trouble in the world.
I know it needs repair.
I hear it and I see the despair,
We focus so much on our own lives & problems.
There is another way to solve them.
If all of God's children did our part,
that would be a great start.
To return to light and make our future bright.
Together we can return to love.

PART 2.
Longing

*This longing that I have for you is
making me do things I wouldn't normally do.
Conjuring thoughts of what could be.
What could have been...*

12 | *You*

Eyes ablaze with the colors of autumn
draw me near

Soulful... full of light and love
Weary from life and loss
Hopeful for what the future holds

Renaissance man, where have you been?
Buried deeply within my heart,
connected to my soul.

Embarking on new territory that screams of old,
familiar, missed opportunity

With hearts wide open
We're living for today
Praying for tomorrow

Laughing together
Smiling together
Dreaming together

Exhale...

Thank you for being
YOU

13 | *Our Dance*

A warm glow
Hand in hand
Electric

Yearning
An ethereal connection
Eternal

Moving
Together as one
Majestic

A forbidden tango
Sweet synchrony
Clandestine

14 | *Blue Steel*

You are with me
even when you're not.
There is no escape.
Though I try to forget,
your face is all I see
in my dreams and when I wake;
soothing me...
quieting my woes.
Your eyes are my sun,
my light source,
my life force,
drawing me into you.
You challenge my mind
and invade my heart.
I'm a moth to your flame.
I cannot resist
and to be honest,
I'd rather not.

15 | *Weekday Lover*

I remember a time not too long ago
when the weekends offered much-anticipated respite.
When TGIF meant "bring it on."
Weekends would fly by and Mondays...
Mondays would come way too soon.

Then you came along,
my weekday lover,
and flipped my world upside down.
Monday through Friday you brought me joy.
Lots of laughs and giant smiles.

Now, these days...
these weekend days drag on
   and on
        and on...
Long days.
Longer nights.
Looking at my phone;
wishing it would ring.
Longing for Mondays,
to hear you sing
Good morning, Baby.
How've you been?

16 | Sparks

What am I to do
when I'm hooked so on you
and you are not mine
to have or to hold?

Truth be told,
you light my fire.
I burn with desire
that cannot be addressed
because I am here
and you are there.

And, well, I'm aware
of all the additional facts
that ensnare our ability to
delight in what feels
so right.

So, I just close my eyes
and allow sparks to fly
in my mind,
reveling in the thoughts of you
that swirl in my head
and warm my heart.

17 | *Wonder*

I wonder if you think of me
as much as I think of you.
I wonder if you'll call.
Wonder if you're ok.
Are they treating you right?
Is today a busy day?
A fun day?
A lonely day?
A joyful day?
I wonder what would make it better?
It's you for me.

When my day is busy,
I want to tell you all about it.
When I'm having a fun day,
I want to laugh with you about it.
When I'm feeling lonely,
I really wish you'd call.
When I'm having a joyful day,
I want to share my joy.

I wonder.
I wonder if someday
this wonder will go away
because you'll be with me.
Not just in my heart and mind,
but also holding my hand
Sharing your world
Making plans
I wonder
and I hope.

18 | *Scarlet Dreams*

My goddess, sensuous and free
cries out to you in the night
Aching for the warmth of your breath on her neck
Longing for the stroke of your hand
on her thighs... up high
Reaching for your face to plant a kiss
on your lips
As wafts of chocolate permeate
all five senses
awakened
Third eyes open
We become one
Musical, rhythmic
We ache to come
But refuse
Not wanting it to end

With the sound of the alarm
I wake
Rejuvenated, ready to seize the day
Knowing
Scarlet dreams await
To quell my soul
Until next time

19 | *Tick Tock*

The count down
is here
3, 2, 1...
Oh, the fun
The twinkle
Sparkle glow
In my eyes
Cannot be denied
Or concealed
It is real.
3, 2, 1...
Blast off
I can't wait to
Blast off with you
To the cosmos, we will go...
With you, I'll go anywhere.

20 | *Stupid*

Why would we subject ourselves to the torture of a
rekindled flame?
A flame that burns so hot
it just won't stop.

Who is to blame?
It is such a shame
how it feels the same,
but like ten times better!
Fresher
Newer
Wanted
Needed
A blessing and a curse
We know... we know...

What if?
What if we let it run its course?
What then?
What comes in the end?
Earth-shattering love?
Long-lasting love?
Broken hearts?
Broken love?
Despair?
Do we care?
Stupid, stupid, stupid.
Do we dare?

21 | *Flirt*

Hey, Cutie
Whatcha doin'?
Lickin' ice cream but
I'd rather be lovin'
Lovin'?
Yeah, Baby
All day long
After you help me slip off
My sweet black thong
Thong?
Yes, Honey
Sweet from that drip
You make me so wet
It drips down my hips
Hips?
Oh, Daddy
I love when you grab 'em
Thrusting so hard
I can taste you
Taste me?
Ahhh, Yes!
Lick me good
So your beautiful body
can slide in smooth
Smooth?
Ya, Darlin'
Like this ice cream I'm lickin'
So soft and creamy

It's got me thinkin'
Thinkin'?
Yeah, Baby
Thinkin' bout what?
About all that good lovin'
I've been missin' so much

22 | *Chocolate*

I once dreamed of chocolate drops
Like raindrops running down the swell of my breasts.

I saw rose petals and bubbles
In my bath and in my glass.

I saw shades of blue swirling alongside
The sound of jazz tickling my ears.

Oh, the dream
So real, indeed.

Who said dreams don't come true?

Not me...

PART 3.
Loving

There is no room for perfection in love, only grace, and understanding.

23 | *Self-Love*

The mirror
Stands tall against the wall
It tells the truth about me

The truth that only I can see
Or maybe God and me
Yes, we both see

Looking deeply into my own eyes
What I see, My Love
Is me, My Love
I love You
My Love

24 | *I Wish You Love*

We spent 20 years together,
18 years raising our beautiful daughter,
17 years committed in marriage,
We've owned 4 houses between us,
Lived in multiple states together,
Owned many cats and a beloved dog,
Endured out-of-state moves and career changes,
Supported each other's dreams.
Share vivid memories,
Like Hamilton close up,
Holiday gatherings,
Christmastime,
Family trips,
Funny jokes,
Movie nights, and much more.
We've managed to get through countless ups and downs.
And now, after all of this time,
I am asking that we be just friends...
To free ourselves
To find ourselves
Because together, we no longer gel.
Better friends than lovers.
Forever connected.
Never forgotten.
No regrets.
I wish you love.

25 | *Puppy Love*

I searched for you
My perfect love
And when I found you
I knew...
You were the one

Easy banter
Hearts aflutter
Lustful looks
Knowing smiles...
I think it was in the eyes

First kiss
Sweet lips
Big...
  and soft...
    and warm...

Decades later
Lives lived apart
Goosebumps and
butterflies impart
Unbridled thoughts...

With you I share
Our unforgettable,
Un-regrettable,
Scintillating
Puppy love

26 | *Soul Love*

You said, 'Look into my eyes.'
And I did with no hesitation.
In your eyes, I saw peace,
solace, pleasure, love, adoration, sex.
In your eyes, I saw sadness, sorrow, confusion,
disappointment, despair.
In your eyes, I saw a plea that I had not seen before.
Your eyes are the gateway to my soul.
Your truth is mine.

27 | *Hot Love*

The temperature in my body burns
Thirsting to be quenched by a love denied
Not to be...
Destined to be apart in the physical,
But connected in spirit to eternity.

The love spills out of you into my cup.
It overflows and I don't know what to do.
All I can do is close my eyes and feel you,
Your soul,
Your spirit
Touching mine.

Thankful to have ever had this most delicious love.

28 | You are Love

When you were created
There was love
When you were understanding
There was love
When you were understood
There was love
When you were worried
There was love
When you were happy
There was love
You are the center of this song
You are made of pure love

29 | *My Baby Love*

Meredith
My one and only
My shining star
My baby

A heart of gold
So sensitive
A smile so bright
It's blinding

Meredith
My greatest gift
My whole world
My baby

A sense of humor
So funny
A style so unique
It's fire

Meredith
My very best friend
You'll always be
My baby

I love you...

30 | *Mother Love*

Mommy
Godsent
Earth Angel
Nurturer
Sugar and spice
A perfect blend
Everything nice
And raw
Mama Bear supreme
A teacher
A healer
My friend
A mother's love
will never end

31 | *Brother Love*

The living, breathing, walking, talking answered prayer
of all those who came before you

A legacy
born to bear your father's name
and fill your mother's heart

The anointed one
Appointed to be
a leader, a trailblazer,
loving son, grandson,
brother...

A formidable branch on
the family tree
Paving the way for those who follow

Brother,
always remember
You are bright
You are strong
You are special
You are loved
You are more than enough

You are everything

32 | New Love

Easy laughter, gentle kisses, missing him.
Safety, warmth, at-homeness in his arms.
Nagging worry at times that it is too early to feel so
close, yet an unmistakable confidence that it is truly real.

Sweetness in his eyes when he looks at me
Lustfully grabbing me, reminding me that I am a woman
first. Worthy of love, desired, appreciated. Savored. I'm
melting.

It may be soon, but I have no doubt
that my soul has been quenched.

33 | *God's Love*

Once upon a time, there was love
Love so strong among man
Now division and scorn
Have forever torn
The fabric of this place we call home
Take heed to your blessings
Bestow love upon your neighbor
It will go far in putting you in God's favor

PART 4.
Light

Shine on...

34 | *Turning Point*

At what point did I lose me
Letting life suck out my energy
Accepting things that did not serve me
Becoming my own enemy

Shrinking myself to avoid conflict
Dimming my light so others might shine
Oh, boy, was I out of line!

I know now who I am
I know now who I shall be
I was created out of love
To be love
To show love
To shine my light for all to see

And guess what...
You will see me!

35 | Homecoming

Sweet anticipation
30 years had passed
A return to the highest of seven hills
where it all began

Who would be there?
What would we do?
Hoping to rekindle old friendships and start some anew

Ready to party
Ready to shine
Ready to strike
One more time

The day finally came.
The moment we arrived
we traveled back in time

A place familiar, yet foreign
Much had changed...
Life happened
But it was the same...
The love sustained.

Homecoming
Coming home to the comforting embrace of FAMUly.

36 | *Awakening*

To see again
To feel again
To love again, so deeply

Transcending time and place
and space

God is mine

37 | *Cleanse*

I close my eyes and travel
Deep within my soul space
Retched and raw from past woes
I caress my sullen heart and
Breathe life into it
Deeply breathing
Inhaling and exhaling
Truth and love and forgiveness
The Breath of Life
Renews and enlightens
I am forgiving
I am forgiven
My heart swells with joy

38 | *The Stillness*

Quiet surrounds me
Thoughts race
Truths exposed
I no longer hesitate
The voices in my head
Divinely led
Bring me to a place
I longed for
The stillness
The silence
The freedom
From this self-inflicted bondage
It's over
Praise God
I'm free

39 | *Voices*

The voices in my head battle for a turn
Hoping to speak to a loved one or friend
The connection to the Great Beyond is strong
The spirit world is truly only a stone's throw away
Be careful what you do during your time on earth
God is watching
You thought being naughty or nice for Santa was a concern
But God!
He sees you
He feels you
All of the time
Be love
Bring love
And you will be fine

40 | *My Soul Says...*

Yes, hallelujah. Be blessed
Sing it loudly—sing
To the top of your lungs—sing
To your soul's delight—sing
Make it great —sing
Sing to the highest heights

Whilst my soul says yes, hallelujah,
I recognize the anguish that it has felt.
Oftentimes drifting
Other times barely afloat
All the time knowing that joy's gonna come
in the morning

I hope that all of God's children know
We have a mighty long way to go and together
it will be done

If our souls say, "yes, hallelujah" to the way
If our souls say, "yes, hallelujah" to the truth
If our souls say, "yes, hallelujah" to the light
If our souls say, "yes, hallelujah" to love

41 | *Saron (Joy)*

Pause and reflect on me,
God says, 'Pause and reflect on me.'
Thine eyes have seen the glory
All the days of her life
She moves with the power of seven winds.
She manifests a world in which love concurs all.
She is bewitched by the notion of it all.
Don't say a word. Speak only with your mind's eye.
See. Feel. Taste. Smell. Hear.
The glory of God.

42 | *God is*

Have you ever looked up at the sky
And thought you saw a bird
And there was no bird there?
Have you ever smelled a loved one
And could not see their face?
Have you ever wanted to be with someone so bad
And you did not understand?
God is love
God is light
God is all around us
God is the waterfall
He is the ocean
He is the trees
He is the mountains
He is the real deal
He is the maker of all
The king of kings
The lord of lords
He is the almighty father
The father of all
The caretaker of the sick
The caretaker of the well
He is the caretaker of the tallest tree
and the deepest valley
He is the light from whom all creatures flow
You came to this earth to do the work of the Lord
You came to this world to show love to your fellow
man

You came to this earth to show that love.... Love... love is the only thing that matters.
Love is the only thing that matters.
Love is the only thing that matters.
Love is the ONLY thing that matters.

43 | *Christ*

What does the word Christ mean to you?
Light, love, salvation.
It's not one person.
It is love. It is in you.
It's all around you.
Believe that.
We are all born with the ability to connect with the
Christ
Within.
Simply ask God to show you the light.

44 | *Light*

Golden tresses frame her face
Eyes so bright and innocent
Her smile delights from near and far

Beauty

She dazzles and explores
Enjoys life and never bores
She is kind most of the time

Beauty

A rare gem with a heart so pure
Conceived in love...

She is the truth
She is the way
She is the light

Beauty

Epilogue
Thank you, God

God,

>Where art thou?
>In the sky;
>On the earth;
>In the sea;
>On a cloud;
>In the deep blue galaxy;
>Or in me?

God,

>I see you in those things and more.
>The swirl of my twirl
>The rose of a bud
>The doo to the wop
>The dew to a drop
>I see you.

God,

>I feel you.
>In the tingle of my heart
>when my love pops by
>From the chill in my bones
>on a cold winter's day
>To the pain of a broken heart

in a most miserable way
I feel you

God

Of the earth
And the moon
And the stars in the sky
Of all of us below
And all of them on high
God, I thank you
For another day
Another moment
To thank you for all you do.

Acknowledgments

When I was lost, I stopped writing for years. Words began to flow again when I was inspired by a spark of joy, thanks to my great friend who will remain nameless for fear that we may get in trouble!

Within a year, I compiled my thoughts in this book; chronicling my path from darkness to light. I found the love of self again, which led to new love, and great hope. I found the light within me! It was a beautiful thing.

I owe this transformation and this compilation to God, the master of my life. He showed up and showed out in a big way for me in 2021 and 2022. For that, I am forever grateful.

In addition, I am beyond thankful to all of the loves of my life, whether they were in my life for a reason, a season, or a lifetime. There are too many people to name. I just hope that they know how much I love them all and how grateful I am for them.

About the Author

Dr. Makeba Morgan Hill, affectionately known as the Doctor of Love, wears many hats as do many women. She is a writer, a Reiki master, a yogi in the making, a health care executive, an entrepreneur, a friend, a mother, a teacher, an extreme cat lover, a believer that children are our future, and a child of God.

Dr. Makeba owns Dr. Makeba & Friends, LLC, which is a holistic wellness center based in Atlanta, Georgia, that specializes in modalities to facilitate balance in the body, mind, and soul for humans and their pets. Using the power of love and light generated through her Reiki energy work and her spiritual connections, she helps souls experience much-needed breakthroughs in all aspects of their lives.

She earned a Bachelor's degree in Healthcare Management from Florida A&M University; a Master of Health Services Administration degree from George Washington University; and a doctorate in higher education from the University of Georgia. A believer in continuing education, she is a Reiki master with certifications in Usui, Karuna Ki, Kundalini, Gold, and Divine Fire methods.

Dr. Makeba is doing her part to bring love and light back to the world. Love is the secret sauce.

Connect with Dr. Makeba:

Website: https://drmakeba4love.com/

Linktree: https://www.linktr.ee/drmakeba4love/

Facebook: https://www.Facebook.com/DrMakeba4Love

Twitter: https://www.Twitter.com/drmakeba4love

YouTube: @DrMakeba4Love

Other Works by the Author

*The Energy Medicine Solution: Mind Blowing Results
for Living and Extraordinary Life*

Chapter 12: Reiki for Love: Igniting the Light in You

*Love Warriors: The Conscious Expert's Guide to
Healing, Joy, and Manifestation*

*Chapter 13: You're Magnetic: Use Reiki Power to
Attract the Love You Need*

Lightning Source UK Ltd.
Milton Keynes UK
UKHW051444260223
417692UK00008B/34